Derbyshire's Lost Railw

by Neil Burgess

The Hathersage Valley.   57. 42.

Hathersage Station is to the left of this view of Hathersage Valley.

Text © Neil Burgess, 2010.
First published in the United Kingdom, 2010,
by Stenlake Publishing Ltd.
01290 551122
www.stenlake.co.uk

ISBN 9781840334999

Printed by
Blissetts, Burgess Road, Acton, W3 8DH

The publishers regret that they cannot supply copies of any pictures featured in this book.

Acknowledgements

I am indebted to my friend and fellow railway historian Richard Morton for reading through the text of this book and suggesting various amendments.

Picture Acknowledgements

The publishers wish to thank the following for contributing photographs to this book:

John Alsop for the front cover, pages 11, 12, 15, 16, 19, 21, 25, 27, 35, 38, 42, 44, 45, 46, 47 (left), 54 and the inside back cover; and Richard Casserley for pages 14, 29, 32, 34, 36 and 39.

Introduction

Though it seems a cliché, Derbyshire is very much a county of contrasting landscapes. The wild open spaces of the Peak District around Buxton and Bakewell, with the ducal seats of Chatsworth and Haddon Hall and the spectacular Derwent gorge at Matlock Bath, seem to have little in common with the open pastures around the Trent further south. Neither appear to have any connection to the mass of collieries and ironworks which once provided employment and a very different way of life for thousands of workers along the Erewash valley, hard up by the county's eastern boundary with Nottinghamshire. Solid, respectable Derby, where Bonny Prince Charlie halted his Jacobites' advance on London in 1745, and fashionable Buxton are very different places to the terraces of Pinxton, Ilkeston, Langley Mill and Clay Cross.

The county's railways developed from these latter industrial centres, the Little Eaton Gangway, horse-worked to the end, being among the first lines in the country. In time, steam-powered railways spread up the river valleys and strode across the hills of the Peak District, linking Derbyshire towns and villages to the cotton-spinners of Manchester, the steel makers and cutlers of Sheffield and, eventually, the commerce and power of London. They created some notable structures, not least the many bridges and stations along the Midland route to Manchester and the inclines and dry stone embankments of the Cromford & High Peak line, which have survived long after the railway itself.

Based in Derby, the Midland certainly stamped its identity on the railways of Derbyshire, but it did not have the county to itself. The Great Northern and Manchester, Sheffield & Lincolnshire companies were eager to exploit the traffic of the coalfield and the minerals of the Peak. When the MS&L (the Great Central after 1899), under its ferocious chairman, Sir Edward Watkin, set its sights not only on London but, through a channel tunnel, on Paris, Berlin and St Petersburg, its line south of Sheffield through Staveley became the first stage of its new route, completed eventually in 1899 as the last new main line in Britain: last, that is, until the rail link between London and the Channel Tunnel was opened in 2007, by which time the Great Central's main line was no longer in existence to connect to it.

The Great Northern's contribution to Derbyshire's railways was more modest than either the Midland's or the MS&L's and little or nothing of it still remains. The same fate has befallen the lines of the lordly London & North Western, which stretched out fingers southwards from Manchester into the uplands of the Peak, reaching Ashbourne in the south and Cromford in the east. The route to Cromford was over the renowned Cromford & High Peak line, celebrated as one of the most singular railways in the country, still worked by a combination of adhesion engines and rope-worked inclined planes until closure in 1967. Today, the last remnant of the LNWR in the county is the line from Stockport to Buxton, which has survived despite all the odds.

Further south, in the low, fertile lands around the Trent and the lower reaches of the Erewash, was situated one of the most fascinating stations in the Midlands. Trent was purely a junction and a place for changing trains, there being no community to serve beyond a few railway staff houses. The line from Nottingham came in from the east, dividing to go up the Erewash valley, across to Derby or to the Derby – Birmingham line at Repton, southwards towards Loughborough, Leicester and London. Triangular junctions to the east and west of Trent meant that it was possible to travel in either direction to go to London, or to Sheffield, a most confusing problem for passengers not 'in the know'; no wonder local schoolchildren changed the words of the Lord's Prayer to ask, '… and lead us not into Trent Station'.

For the railway enthusiast, though, Trent offered the spectacle of passenger and goods trains passing through day and night, long loaded coal trains – often hauled in later days by London Midland & Scottish 'Garratt' articulated locomotives – sweeping down off the flying junctions which allowed traffic from the Erewash valley to cross the passenger lines unimpeded.

Derby itself offered the prospect not only of a busy station, dealing with traffic to the north of England through Sheffield, to London through Leicester or Nottingham, or to the west through Tamworth and Birmingham, but also the locomotive, carriage and wagon works, the spiritual home of the Midland Railway. The line north to Chesterfield – the North Midland Railway – had been engineered by no less a figure than George Stephenson, the archetypal early Victorian self-made man, who lived in the grand Tapton House at Chesterfield, along the route of the line. The line to Birmingham linked Derby not only to 'the city of a thousand trades' but to the line from there that went south towards Gloucester and Bristol. The Birmingham & Derby Junction and North Midland lines formed the nucleus of the Midland, which eventually stretched its routes to the four points of the compass, reaching Carlisle and Swansea over its own metals and Cromer and Bournemouth by way of joint lines. Yet even when it opened its new London Extension in 1868, the Midland remained a provincial railway at heart and many of its routes had their lineside distances measured from London Road Junction at Derby.

The Midland's locomotive, carriage and wagon works at Derby was one of the great centres of the railway age, not only in the steam era but also into the modern period. During the 1930s it lost pride of place on the London, Midland & Scottish system to a reinvigorated Crewe, but during that decade the LMS established its technical research section and its school of transport there. Later, in the 1960s, British Railways added the experimental testing station, which undertook a variety of important design projects, including the High Speed Train – undoubtedly one of the greatest successes of the diesel era – as well as the ill-starred tilting Advanced Passenger Train. In the great bargain sell-off of rail privatisation, Derby works became the base for Bombardier Transport, one of the few remaining producers of trains and rolling stock in Britain.

Derbyshire has fared well in the railway preservation era, with two active steam railways – the Midland Railway Centre at Butterley and Peak Rail at Matlock – while the Ecclesbourne Valley Railway, on part of the former Wirksworth branch, offers a third example of preservation. The limestone of the Peak District has provided a healthy traffic in aggregates to compensate for the almost total disappearance of coal, whilst the Midland routes from Sheffield through Derby to Bristol and to London are two of the great rail arteries of Britain. Elsewhere, routes through the Peak District National Park, particularly those from Buxton to Ashbourne and over the Cromford & High Peak line, though long devoid of trains, have been adapted to become long-distance walking and cycle paths.

Derbyshire offers the student of railway history a fascinating insight into the varieties of the Victorian age of transport and industry. It is hoped that this book may evoke some of the scenes now long gone as a tribute to what was once the everyday business of travel.

Cromford – Whaley Bridge

Passenger services withdrawn   1877 (precise date unknown)
Distance   33 miles
Company   Cromford & High Peak Railway

Passengers were carried between Cromford and Whaley Bridge from before 1855, possibly from 1843. The service was cut back from Cromford to Ladmanlow in 1856 and ceased in 1877. No stations are recorded.

Cromford Station, which is still open, August 1958.

In their earliest days, railways were often built as feeders to the established network of canals and navigable rivers, rather than as transport systems in their own right. They were often constructed in a similar manner to canals with level, or nearly level, sections interspersed with inclined planes. Horses worked the level sections and stationary winding engines hauled carriages and wagons up the inclines; even when steam locomotives arrived on the scene they were often insufficiently reliable to haul loads up gradients and the inclined planes remained.

The lower-lying areas around the Peak District had canals by the early nineteenth century, but the high limestone uplands were too steep and the bedrock too porous for them. So, in May 1825, a railway – or 'Tram Road' – was authorised by Parliament to connect the Cromford Canal at Cromford to the Peak Forest Canal at Whaley Bridge, then just inside Cheshire. The route was to include nine inclined planes, of up to 1 in 7, along with more level horse-worked sections. The section from Cromford to Hurdlow opened in May 1830 and the remainder, to Whaley Bridge, in July 1831.

The Cromford & High Peak Railway served as a canal feeder – and an important link in the route from east to west across the lower end of the Pennines – until a connection was laid to the Manchester, Buxton, Matlock & Midlands Junction Railway line at High Peak Junction in 1853. In the skirmishing with the Midland about the latter's attempts to build a route to Manchester, the London & North Western leased the C&HP in 1862, absorbing it in 1887.

Steam locomotives arrived on the line in 1833, though it took three decades for them to oust horse haulage on the route. The development of more powerful locomotives allowed the route to be reconstructed in places, easing some of the very sharp curves and realigning some of the inclines so that they could be worked by locomotives; Hurdlow incline, for example, was reduced from 1 in 16 to 1 in 60 in 1855. As noted above, during this period passengers were carried over the line, though this was in a coach attached to the rear of the goods trains, the passengers having to get out and walk up or down the inclines – the journey from Whaley Bridge to Cromford taking around six hours, not very much faster than walking. A fatal accident in 1877 led to the withdrawal of the passenger service.

Acquisition by the LNWR in 1887 led to the abandonment of the northern end of the line in June 1892, the route being replaced by the new line from Buxton to Ashbourne, which actually incorporated parts of the C&HP between Parsley Hay and Ladmanlow. This allowed the abandonment of three of the original inclines, Bunsall, Shallcross and Whaley Bridge, so that by the end of the nineteenth century there were just two worked by stationary engines, Sheep Pasture (maximum gradient 1 in 8) and Middleton (1 in 8¼). Hurdlow had been reduced to 1 in 60, while Hopton, with a maximum gradient of 1 in 14, was the steepest worked by adhesion locomotives in Britain. Sheep Pasture and Middleton were balanced inclines, where the weight of loaded wagons going down was countered by that of empties going up, the stationary engines being more for braking than haulage.

The Cromford & High Peak served its remote peakland quarries for most of seven decades of the twentieth century; it also had other uses, not least the supply of drinking water to remote peakland farms and houses. Although in many ways an anachronism, in the age before heavy lorries roaring along peakland roads it was the most efficient means of carrying the heavy loads. After the Second World War it became a magnet for railway enthusiasts, many of whom arranged special excursions in goods brake vans or even open wagons, to savour its route, stopping to watch and photograph former North London Railway and later BR J94 'Austerity' 0-6-0 tank engines storming Hopton incline. In June 1963 the line ceased to be a through route when Middleton incline was closed. The end came on 30 April 1967, witnessed by crowds in the blustery spring weather. The trackbed still remains, converted into the High Peak Trail for walkers and cyclists, while the winding engine house at Middleton Top has been restored.

Matlock – Chinley

Passenger services withdrawn	6 March 1967
Distance	26 miles
Company	Manchester, Buxton, Matlock & Midlands Junction Railway / Ambergate – Rowsley: Midland Railway

Stations closed	*Date*
Matlock Bath *	6 March 1967
Matlock **	6 March 1967
Darley Dale ***	6 March 1967
Rowsley ****	6 March 1967
Bakewell	6 March 1967
Hassop †	17 August 1942
Great Longstone for Ashford ††	10 September 1962
Monsal Dale	10 August 1959

Miller's Dale †††	6 March 1967
Peak Forest ††††	6 March 1967
Chapel-en-le-Frith Central ‡	6 March 1967

* Reopened on 27 May 1972.

** Named Matlock Bridge until 1 July 1905; reopened on 27 May 1972.

** Named Darley until 1 October 1890.

**** Named Rowsley for Chatsworth between 1 September 1867 and 14 June 1965.

† Named Hassop for Chatsworth between *c*.1870 and *c*.1906.

†† Named Longstone until 1 October 1913.

††† Named Miller's Dale for Tideswell between 1 May 1889 and 14 June 1965.

†††† Named Peak Forest for Peak Dale between 26 September 1893 and 14 June 1965.

‡ Named Chapel-en-le-Frith until 2 June 1924.

Matlock Station, 1957.

Great Longstone Station.

During the nineteenth century, Manchester was a place of phenomenal wealth, in the vanguard of technological and civic progress. It had been the terminus of the first ever railway built purposely for the carriage of both passengers and goods – Stephenson's Liverpool & Manchester line – and it is hardly surprising that later companies sought to reach it to carry its lucrative products. The Midland Railway, expanding its territory throughout the 1850s and 1860s, sought a route from its Derby – Leeds line across the country to 'Cottonopolis', but was threatened in its plans by the London & North Western, already firmly ensconced in Manchester and equally anxious to keep out potential rivals.

Miller's Dale Station, 1957.

The 1840s, the period known to history as the 'Railway Mania', saw a great many speculative schemes for new railways. Much of what was proposed was impractical and even impossible to construct, but there were lines which had genuine potential. One such was the comprehensively named Manchester, Buxton, Matlock & Midlands Junction Railway, which in 1845 proposed a line from Manchester across the Peak District to Ambergate, on the North Midland line between Derby and Chesterfield, where it would make an end-on junction with the proposed Ambergate, Nottingham & Boston & Eastern Junction Railway. The line would leave Manchester and proceed through Stockport and Whaley Bridge to Buxton; then through Miller's Dale, down the Wye Valley to Rowsley, and thence to Ambergate along the valley of the Derwent.

Miller's Dale Station, August 1958.

The 'Railway Mania', like all fits of speculation, eventually lost momentum and many of its schemes were either stillborn or else collapsed into insolvency. The Manchester, Buxton, Matlock & Midlands Junction had managed to gain Parliamentary approval, but then began considering alternative routes, one of which was to continue up the Derwent Valley from Rowsley towards Chatsworth before entering the Wye Valley near Hassop. While the line from Ambergate was opened as far as Rowsley, along the way connecting Matlock to the national network on 4 June 1849, there it was destined to end for some years. The Duke of Devonshire was decidedly opposed to any railway near Chatsworth, so further thinking was necessary. In the meantime the Midland and the LNWR jointly leased the line to Rowsley, the Midland hoping to go on to Manchester and the LNWR equally anxious to prevent it. In 1852, the LNWR supported a line to Whaley Bridge from Stockport and four years later promoted an extension to Buxton in the hope of blocking the Midland. In so doing, it not only overstretched itself financially, but also incurred the opposition of the Manchester, Sheffield & Lincolnshire Railway. In 1860 the Midland gained authorisation to extend from Rowsley to Buxton and from there gained access to Manchester through Peak Forest and New Mills over a line backed by the MS&LR.

PEAK DALE STATION. 415

The Midland's route opened throughout to Manchester on 1 February 1867 and rapidly established itself as one of the great scenic routes in Britain, traversing the spectacular landscape of the Peak District. Not everyone was pleased at its intrusion, and the philosopher John Ruskin famously poured scorn and derision on what he saw as the desecration of the wild countryside, particularly around Miller's Dale. The Duke of Rutland, whose estate at Haddon Hall had admitted the railway, nevertheless insisted that it should run in a tunnel so as not to interfere with the view, though he may have found the connection for London at Bakewell a convenience. The Midland went to great pains and cost to construct solid buildings and structures intended to blend into their surroundings and many of them remain, long after the trains have gone.

A 4-4-0 locomotive, No. 728, at Chapel-en-le-Frith.

10 2 A.M. EXPRESS, MID. STATION, CHAPEL-EN-LE-FRITH.

The Midland route through the Peak was never particularly fast due to stiff gradients and an abundance of curves. Goods trains toiling up to Manchester received banking assistance from Rowsley, where the engine shed survived until January 1965. The Beeching Report saw the route as an unnecessary duplication of the line from Chinley to Sheffield along the Hope Valley and, in March 1967, the section between Peak Forest and Matlock was closed for local traffic, through traffic ceasing entirely from 1 July 1968. However, since then the section between Matlock and Rowsley has been restored as a steam railway, Peak Rail, with the ultimate intention of reopening the route all the way to Buxton.

Miller's Dale – Buxton

Passenger services withdrawn	6 March 1967	*Stations closed*	*Date*
Distance	4 miles	Blackwell Mill	6 March 1967
Company	Midland Railway	Buxton	6 March 1967

Midland Railway's Buxton Station, 1948.

The dukes of Devonshire owned considerable estates in Derbyshire and during the later eighteenth century were instrumental in developing Buxton as a spa town where rich and fashionable people could come to 'take the waters'. As discussed earlier, there was an understandable wish by railway promoters that any line crossing the Peak District should serve the town and the first to gain authorisation to do so was the Stockport, Disley & Whaley Bridge Railway, a client of the LNWR, in 1854. The original Midland main line authorised in 1860 was between Rowsley and Buxton, though two years later the connection to Manchester via New Mills and Chinley meant that this would effectively become the main route with the line from Miller's Dale to Buxton as a branch.

Buxton thereby not only gained service by two railways, but their stations were built next door to one another and, even more unusually, in an identical style. They also opened on the same day, 30 May 1863, the Duke of Devonshire having supported both routes. In many ways the two lines offered complementary services, the LNWR being most convenient for travel to Manchester while the Midland was better for passengers going to Derby or London. The line even boasted what was reputed to be the smallest public station in Britain, at Blackwell Mill, constructed for the use of the families of railway staff housed nearby. The closure of the Midland route from Rowsley effectively sealed the fate of the Miller's Dale to Buxton service and it was withdrawn on the same day. Although there has been an attempt to reopen the line to Rowsley, the Midland station has been demolished apart from the base of its decorative end wall, though the LNWR one remains as a terminus for services to Stockport and Manchester.

Duffield – Wirksworth

		Stations closed	Date
Passenger services withdrawn	16 June 1947	Hazlewood	16 June 1947
Distance	9 miles	Shottle	16 June 1947
Company	Midland Railway	Idridgehay	16 June 1947
		Wirksworth	16 June 1947

The 7.55 p.m. service from Duffield to Wirksworth at Hazlewood Station, 27 June 1933.

As described earlier, the Midland Railway eventually built its main line through the Peak District from Rowsley to Chinley during the 1870s, but since this involved the purchase of a line in which the LNWR had a share, this was by no means a foregone conclusion. In the meantime the Midland sought to project an alternative route a little further south and this involved the construction of a branch line up the Ecclesbourne Valley from Duffield to Wirksworth. Although there was a good deal of potential traffic from Wirksworth, particularly in stone and milk, the possibility of extending the line and transforming it into a main route to Manchester existed. In the event this never happened and the Wirksworth line remained a branch.

Idridgehay Station, *c*.1907.

The line opened to passenger traffic in October 1867 and to goods in December. Although it joined the main line north of Derby at Duffield, trains ran to and from Derby rather than the junction. The route led an uneventful existence under the Midland and passed to the London, Midland & Scottish Railway at the Grouping in 1923. The coal shortage caused the LMS to withdraw the passenger service in June 1947, just six months before the company was nationalised and absorbed into British Railways, though excursion trains for walkers and visitors to the Derbyshire Dales continued into the 1960s. Goods facilities at Idridgehay and Hazlewood were withdrawn from January 1953 and stone traffic, a staple of the line, ceased in 1959, but Shottle continued to send and receive goods until March 1964. Wirksworth itself closed finally in April 1968. Attempts have been made to reopen the line since closure, the first being made by Wyvern Rail in 1992, but it took until 2005 for the Ecclesbourne Valley Railway Association to recommence a service on the section from Wirksworth to Gursey Bank.

A 4-4-0T locomotive, No. 10, at Wirksworth Station. It was on loan from the Midland & Great Northern Joint Railway and the coach was a former Pullman car.

In its later days, Wirksworth was used as an attractive location for taking the official photographs of the four former Midland locomotives – Kirtley 2-4-0 No. 158A, Johnson 4-2-2 No. 118, Deeley compound No. 1000 and 'Tilbury tank' No.79 *Thundersley* – which were preserved as part of the National Collection and stored at Derby locomotive works during the 1960s.

Wirksworth Station, 27 June 1953.

Ashbourne – Buxton

Passenger services withdrawn	1 November 1954	Alsop-en-le-Dale	1 November 1954
Distance	22¼ miles	Hartington	1 November 1954
Company	London & North Western Railway	Parsley Hay	1 November 1954
		Hurdlow *	15 August 1949
		Hindlow	1 November 1954
Stations closed	*Date*	Higher Buxton	2 April 1951
Ashbourne	1 November 1954		
Thorpe Cloud	1 November 1954		
Tissington	1 November 1954	* Closed between December 1877 and 1 June 1894.	

Ashbourne Station.

The Peak District owes its landscape to the bedrock on which it stands, principally limestone. Its characteristics as an easily worked and attractive building stone made it much valued during the eighteenth and nineteenth centuries, while the twentieth century saw an increased interest in limestone aggregates as hardcore material for road and other construction projects. It was the hope of tapping traffic from quarries in north-west Derbyshire that prompted the London & North Western Railway to reconstruct the western end of the Cromford & High Peak line, discussed earlier, and to strike out southwards towards the ancient market town of Ashbourne. A rail connection to Ashbourne from the south had existed since May 1852, provided by the North Staffordshire Railway's branch off the Churnet Valley line at Rocester. When the LNWR line arrived in Ashbourne on 4 August 1899, it was into a new station jointly owned by the two companies, the original North Staffordshire station being closed at the same time.

Alsop-en-le-Dale Station.

If the quarry traffic was promising, passengers numbers were much less so, the villages along the line being very small and isolated. Paradoxically, the LNWR had maintained a regular service of through coaches from Buxton to Euston up to 1917, trains running south via Nuneaton. Seasonal traffic was provided by ramblers and during the winters, which could be severe, the train provided a vital link with the outside world, but neither was sufficient to maintain the regular passenger service beyond November 1954. Even so, occasional passenger excursions continued to operate until 7 October 1963, along with special services when winter weather was severe, the last being during the notorious 'Great Freeze' of 1962/63.

Higher Buxton Station, 1948.

Goods traffic continued over the northern section of the line until 1967, when the closure of the Cromford & High Peak line ended regular workings of stone. The track was lifted, but in 1969 the Peak Park Planning Board acquired the trackbed south of Hartington to convert it into a cycle and walking path, the Tissington Trail. However, stone traffic still continues over the northern end between Hindlow and Buxton.

Ilkeston – Derby – Egginton Junction

Passenger services withdrawn	see *Stations closed*	Mickleover	4 December 1939
Distance	16½ miles	Etwall	4 December 1939
Company	Great Northern Railway	Egginton Junction ***	6 March 1962

Stations closed	*Date*
Ilkeston North *	7 September 1964
West Hallam	7 September 1964
Breadsall	6 April 1953
Derby Friargate **	7 September 1964

* Named Ilkeston until 1 July 1950.
** Named Derby until December 1881.
*** Great Northern & North Staffordshire joint station, opened on 1 July 1878 to replace Egginton Station which was 400 metres west.

Ilkeston Station.

West Hallam Station, 1963.

The Great Northern Railway owned a good deal of railway in the east Midlands, though its main areas of operation were probably the West Riding of Yorkshire, Lincolnshire and the corridor of lines coming off the East Coast main line between Doncaster and London. The company was keen to open up routes penetrating into the territory of its rivals, particularly the Midland and London & North Western, and the line described here formed part of a route which gave it access to the west Midlands, crossing the Midland Railway's home ground and eventually ending in the LNWR station in Stafford. At its eastern end the line made a connection with the route from Grantham to Nottingham, running around the eastern and northern edges of the city – as the Nottingham Suburban Railway – towards the industrial area straddling the boundary between Nottinghamshire and Derbyshire. It then continued to Derby and on to Egginton Junction where it made a connection with the North Staffordshire Railway's line from Derby to Stoke.

West Hallam Station, 1963.

Running powers over the NSR gave access to Uttoxeter, from where the Great Northern gained its own line to Stafford, while similar running powers gave access to Burton-on-Trent over the triangular junction at Rolleston on the Tutbury – Burton line. Much of the planning of these Great Northern lines, and the branches from them to Pinxton, Heanor and Stanton, was undertaken in 1872 and the goal was the lucrative traffic from the developing coalfield. Goods services began to run through to Burton in January 1878, passenger trains starting in April. The Stafford & Uttoxeter line had been worked by the Great Northern from 1867 and it was eventually absorbed in 1881.

Derby Friargate Station, 1964.

The network lasted into the 1930s, but from the early months of the Second World War it began to contract from its western end. The Stafford – Uttoxeter line lost its passenger service in 1939 along with the stations west of Derby, though through the 1950s services continued to Friargate from Nottingham. The end came in the early 1960s, though parts of the network continued to see goods traffic after this and the bridge at the exit to Friargate Station is not only still there but carefully repainted.

Kimberley – Heanor

Passenger services withdrawn	4 December 1939	*Stations closed*	*Date*
Distance	4¼ miles (Ilkeston –	Marlpool *	30 April 1928
	Heanor)	Heanor *	30 April 1928
Original owning company	Great Northern Railway		

* Closed to regular public services from this date, though workmen's trains continued until 4 December 1939.

Heanor Station, 1948.

The Great Northern promoted a line to Heanor to rival that of the Midland by extending its line from Kimberly, which had originally served Nutbrook colliery at Shipley. The new passenger line opened on 1 July 1891, trains being worked from Ilkeston, and in 1910 there were nine return journeys a day, though no Sunday service. The intermediate station at Marlpool closed in 1928 and the passenger service ended at the same time as the closure of the Derby – Egginton Junction and Stafford line in December 1939. Goods traffic continued for more than twenty years more, finally ending in 1963.

Kimberley – Pinxton *

Passenger services withdrawn	7 January 1963	*Stations closed*	*Date*
Distance	8½ miles	Pinxton **	7 January 1963
Original owning company	Great Northern Railway		

Pinxton South Station, 11 August 1964.

* The closed stations on this line that were in Nottinghamshire were Newthorpe, Eastwood & Langley Mill, Codnor Park and Pye Hill & Somercotes.

** Renamed Pinxton South from January 1954.

Although the town of Pinxton is in Derbyshire, this Great Northern branch off the 'back line' from Kimberley was in Nottinghamshire, more or less following the county boundary throughout its length. Coal was the principal reason for building it, but the passenger traffic kept going until the end, goods facilities also being withdrawn on the day the passenger service ceased. The route was duplicated along its whole length by the Midland Railway's Erewash Valley line, though the Great Northern line was credited with having stations which were generally thought to be better placed for the communities they served.

Tutbury – Burton-on-Trent *

Passenger services withdrawn	13 June 1960	**Stations closed**	**Date**
Distance	5½ miles	Rolleston-on-Dove	1 January 1949
Company	North Staffordshire Railway	Stretton & Clay Mills	1 January 1949

* The closed station on this line that was in Staffordshire was Horninglow.

Stretton & Clay Mills Station.

The coming of railways made a considerable difference to the brewing of beer in Britain. Whereas before beer was brewed locally, often by farmers or innkeepers, and consumed locally within days, rail transport, and the use of hops which kept the beer fresh for longer, allowed the creation of much larger breweries, serving wider areas. Burton-on-Trent, situated where the river forms the boundary between Staffordshire and Derbyshire, developed as one of the great brewing centres in England, its products being distributed all over the country. The Midland Railway almost managed to keep Burton to itself, but could not prevent the North Staffordshire, with which it enjoyed cordial relations and mutual running powers, from building a connection from its Derby – Stoke line at Tutbury into the town. The original route, from Stoke via Uttoxeter, was originally the destination of the traffic and opened to passengers on 11 September 1848, and to goods exactly a year later. The Burton services were later operated separately from the junction at Tutbury, in LMS days by push-pull trains.

The 'Tutbury Jenny' called originally at three intermediate stations – Rolleston, Stretton and Horninglow; although these closed on New Year's Day 1949, the 'Jenny' ran until 1960. Tutbury Station closed on 7 November 1966, but during the 1990s a new station opened near the site of the old one, served by trains between Derby and Stoke.

Ilkeston Junction – Ilkeston Town

Passenger services withdrawn	16 June 1947 (see text)	*Stations closed*	*Date*
Distance	¾ mile	Ilkeston Town *	16 June 1947
Company	Midland Railway		

* Named Ilkeston until 2 May 1870.

Railways in Derbyshire, like those in many industrial areas, were initially built to move coal and other minerals more easily and quickly than either by road or canal. This was the impetus to construct the line running from Trent up the Erewash valley, which opened to Codnor Park on 6 September 1847. Indeed, such was the Midland Railway's desire to capture the coal traffic for the Leicester market that the line bypassed the lace and hosiery-making town of Ilkeston, so passengers wishing to travel by train needed to take the ¾ mile branch line to Ilkeston Junction on the main line. Even after providing a connection, the Midland's services were not well received, many Ilkeston people preferring to walk to the junction. In 1870 the company closed the branch to passengers altogether, but reopened it from the 1 July 1879. In later years the line was served by trains running down the main Erewash valley line, which involved the train engine running round its train twice. Not surprisingly, this was a relatively lengthy process, though there were eighteen departures from the Town station in the 1938 timetable. The service survived the war, but – as with the Wirksworth and Pye Bridge – Ambergate branches and some other lines elsewhere in the country – was suspended during the fuel crisis of 1947, never to be reinstated. The closure was made permanent by British Railways from 10 July 1950. Goods traffic continued until 15 June 1959.

Ripley – Derby via Kilburn (Ripley branch)

Passenger services withdrawn	1 June 1930	Kilburn	1 June 1930
Distance	10 miles (Ripley – Derby)	Coxbench	1 June 1930
Company	Midland Railway	Little Eaton	1 June 1930
Stations closed	*Date*		
Ripley *	1 June 1930	* This replaced the first station on 2 September 1889.	
Denby **	1 June 1930	** Named Smithy Houses until 1 November 1856 when it was renamed as Denbey. Renamed again on 1 February 1878.	

The three branches between the Erewash valley and North Midland lines considered here formed a network of short lines which opened up the area around Ripley to rail communications with the wider world. The first, between Ripley and the North Midland line at Little Eaton Junction, was authorised by the Midland Railway (Ripley Branches) Act of 1848 and extended an existing line to Little Eaton which served several quarries and made a connection with the Erewash Canal. The aim of the line was to develop the traffic in coal and minerals from the area around Ripley and it was this traffic, rather than passengers, which sustained it over the years. Passenger services were fairly sparse, amounting in 1910, the zenith of the railway age, to only six return journeys on most weekdays with two extras on Saturdays. In 1889 a new station was opened at Ripley, replacing the earlier structure. The passenger service managed to survive the Great War, but succumbed in the depths of the Depression in June 1930. Goods traffic continued for at least another 35 years, the southern section to Denby closing altogether in August 1977. The Little Eaton – Derby section eventually closed during the 1990s and at the time of writing the track is still *in situ*.

Locomotive No. 1365 at Ripley with the 8.50 a.m. service from Derby, 7 June 1926.

Holbrook level crossing near Coxbench Station, 1967.

Little Eaton Station, 1948.

Pye Bridge – Ambergate

Passenger services withdrawn	16 June 1947	*Stations closed*	*Date*
Distance	6½ miles	Butterley *	16 June 1947
Company	Midland Railway		

* Renamed Butterley for Ripley and Swanwick on 29 July 1935. Reopened and renamed as Butterley on 22 August 1981.

Butterley, looking towards Pye Bridge, 3 September 1955.

The second of the branches between the Erewash valley and North Midland lines, the section from Pye Bridge to Ambergate was authorised by the Midland Railway (New Lines and Additional Powers) Act of 1865, opened to mineral traffic in June 1874, and to passengers in February of the following year. The passenger service was fairly frequent, six return journeys along the length of the line in 1910, plus more which ran to and from Butterley only. It survived the Second World War, but was withdrawn in the last year of the LMS's independent existence due to the fuel crisis, a little more than six months before nationalisation. Goods traffic continued into the late 1960s, but after closure part of the line was revived as the Midland Railway Centre, run by the Midland Railway Trust. As such it still sees regular trains, both steam and diesel.

Butterley – Shipley Gate

Passenger services withdrawn	2 January 1967	*Stations closed*	*Date*
Distance	6½ miles (Langley Mill – Butterley)	Crosshill & Codnor *	4 May 1926
		Heanor *	4 May 1926
Company	Midland Railway		

* Closed between 1 January 1917 and 3 May 1920.

This is the third of the routes between the Erewash valley and North Midland lines, authorised by the Midland Railway (Additional Powers) act of 1884, for the Crosshill – Butterley section, and from 1886, for the section from Crosshill to the Erewash valley line north of Shipley Gate at Heanor goods junction. Once again, the passenger services succumbed early, having fought a losing battle with electric street tramways in the early years of the twentieth century. During the Great War they were suspended between January 1917 and May 1920, only to be suspended again during the General Strike of 1926 and never subsequently reinstated. Final goods services ended in 1963, though Heanor lost its goods service in 1951. Closeness to both the Erewash valley line and the Great Northern's Pinxton branch can hardly have helped matters, but once again mineral traffic was probably the company's main objective.

Pear Tree & Normanton – Ashby-de-la-Zouch, including the Melbourne Military Railway *

Passenger services withdrawn	22 September 1930	* The closed stations on this line that were in Leicestershire were Tonge & Breedon and Worthington.
Distance	14¾ miles	** Named Chellaston until 15 June 1901. Reopened and renamed as Chellaston on 17 May 1959.
Company	Midland Railway	

Stations closed	*Date*
Chellaston & Swarkstone **	22 September 1930
Melbourne	22 September 1930

The Midland line between Pear Tree & Normanton (on the main line from Derby to Birmingham through Burton-on-Trent) to Ashby-de-la-Zouch (on the Leicester – Burton line) had several interesting features, even though to a casual observer it was simply a rural byway. It had originally been promoted in several sections, that from Pear Tree to Melbourne opening on 1 September 1868 as a newly constructed line, whereas the section south to Ashby was a conversion of the 4' 2" gauge horse-worked tramway linking Cloud Hill lime works at Breedon to the Ashby canal, which had originally opened in April 1799. The Midland hoped to benefit from the quarry traffic along the route and also from market gardening in the Ashby area, though it seemed not to hold out great hopes for the passenger service. These expectations were broadly confirmed by the line's subsequent receipts and the passenger service was particularly affected by the introduction of buses in the area after the Great War. This was eventually withdrawn on 22 September 1930.

Chellaston Station, 22 May 1965.

On the outbreak of war in September 1939, there was a recognition that, as in the Great War, military railways would play a key role in moving troops, weapons and supplies. In 1906 the Royal Engineers had set up a military training railway at Longmoor in Hampshire, near the garrison of Bordon; this was originally named the Woolmer Instructional Military Railway, the name changing to the Longmoor Military Railway in 1935. Thousands of military railwaymen were trained at Longmoor over the decades, but in 1939 its capacity was less than the Army required. This had been recognised by Colonel Manton, the Principal of the LMS School of Transport in Derby, who suggested that the Engineers should take over the Ashby line for the duration of the war as a 'second Longmoor'. Thus, on 19 November 1939, the line passed into the hands of the Army as No. 2 Railway Training Centre, Melbourne.

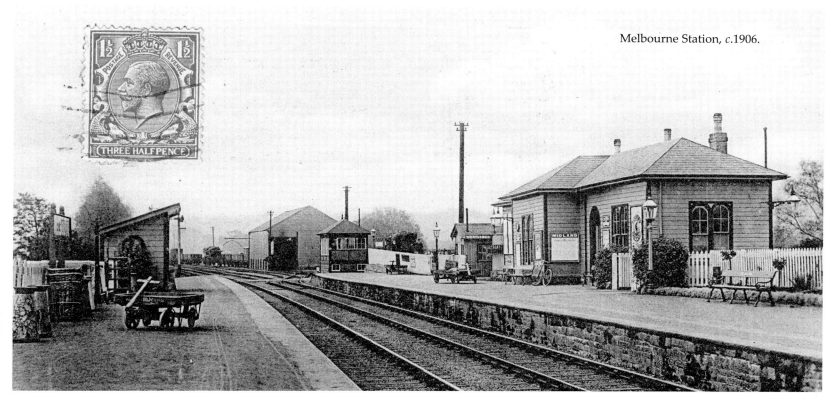

Melbourne Station, *c*.1906.

During the war the military authorities maintained the goods service along the line, but also dramatically extended its facilities to cope with a huge volume of supplies and material which was assembled for campaigns throughout the conflict. The soldiers also constructed a series of prefabricated bridges along the route as practice for similar activities in theatres of war. After the United States entered the war in December 1941, American military railwaymen also used the line for training. After D-Day, allied forces were rapidly deployed in Europe and extensive stock piles of stores assembled for the invasion were no longer required; the military railway units also moved overseas to repair and maintain the railways in the wake of the allied advance into Germany. From 1 January 1945, the LMS resumed full control of the line.

The line continued as a through route until 1955, when the southern section into Ashby was closed. Tonge and Breedon closed to goods in 1959, Worthington in 1964, and Chellaston & Swarkestone in 1966. The final section of the line operated from Lount colliery to supply coal to Drakelow power station until 1968, after which the line was operated as an elongated siding from Worthington Junction to allow movement of occasional loads of limestone. Final closure came on 21 May 1980.

Clay Cross and Ashover

		Stations closed	Date
Passenger services withdrawn	14 September 1936	Clay Cross & Edstow	14 September 1936
Distance	7¼ miles	Chesterfield Road	14 September 1936
Company	Ashover Light Railway	Stretton	14 September 1936
		Woolley	14 September 1936
		Fallgate	14 September 1936
		Ashover Butts	14 September 1936

Locomotive 'Joan' at Stretton Station, 16 September 1930.

Unlike parts of north Wales and much of rural Ireland, narrow gauge railways were not common in England and they tended to arrive late on the scene and close quickly. One such was the Ashover Light Railway, constructed by the Clay Cross Company, an undertaking which owed its origins to George Stephenson who retired to the area in the 1840s. The company was involved in iron-making and quarrying in that part of Derbyshire and the line was built to serve the quarries.

A 4-6-0T locomotive, 'Bridget', at Fallgate Station.

Ashover Butts, 1926.

Terminus of Ashover Light Railway at The Butts, Ashover.

'Joan' at Ashover Butts,
23 October 1926.

The First World War had required vast networks of light railways to supply the armies of both sides, the British using either home-produced locomotives and rolling stock or material supplied from the USA. After the war the government disposed of the railways and the Clay Cross Company acquired their locomotives and rolling stock from this source, including six two-foot gauge 4-6-0 tank engines built by Baldwins in Philadelphia. The line was surveyed by the redoubtable Colonel Holman Fred Stephens, whose involvement with impecunious light railways in the years between the wars is the stuff of legend. Construction was authorised in 1919 and the line opened on 6 April 1925. Although mainly for mineral traffic, the ALR carried passengers in its early days, mostly local people and walkers exploring the scenery of the Amber Valley. The year-round passenger service ceased in 1934 and the summer-only trains continued until 1936, killed off by road competition. The mineral workings continued through the Second World War and finally ceased on 31 March 1950. In recent years the Ashover Light Railway Society have devised plans to reinstate the section between Ashover Butts and Dark Lane as a steam railway.

Sheffield – Nottingham *

Passenger services withdrawn	3 September 1966	Renishaw Central ****	4 March 1963
Distance	38¼ miles	Staveley Central †	4 March 1963
Company	Manchester, Sheffield &	Brimington ††	2 January 1956
	Lincolnshire Railway	Chesterfield Central	4 March 1963
	(Great Central Railway from 1899)	Grassmoor	4 October 1940
		Heath	4 March 1963
Stations closed	*Date*	Pilsley	2 November 1959
Beighton **	1 November 1954	Tibshelf Town	4 March 1963
Killamarsh Central ***	4 March 1963		

Killamarsh Station.

* Closed stations on this line that were in Nottinghamshire were Kirkby Bentinck, Hollin Well & Annesley, Hucknall Central, Bulwell Common, New Basford and Carrington.
** Closed between February 1852 and March 1854. Replaced by the Great Central's station of the same name, 120 metres south-east, on 1 November 1893.
*** Named Killamarsh until 25 September 1950.
**** Named Eckington & Renishaw until 25 September 1950.
† Named Staveley Town until 25 September 1950.
†† Named Sheepbridge & Brimington until 18 June 1951.

Chesterfield is Derbyshire's historic second town and was a place of some importance throughout the eighteenth century as a market for lead and iron. It was first linked to the rail network by means of George Stephenson's North Midland Railway between Derby and Leeds, opened as far as Masborough on 11 May 1840 and later incorporated into the Midland Railway. However, the Manchester, Sheffield & Lincolnshire Railway was interested in gaining access to the coalfield from the north and, after abortive negotiation with the Midland for access over their lines broke down, promoted a bill through Parliament in 1889.

Eckington & Renishaw Station.

Up to 1894 the MS&L constructed a line from Beighton, near Sheffield, through Chesterfield to Annesley in Nottinghamshire, colliery branches being constructed as the line progressed. Chesterfield was first served by MS&L passenger trains on 4 June 1892 and, on 2 January 1893, was linked by the company to Nottingham London Road via Staveley Town, access to Nottingham being by running powers over the Great Northern from Annesley.

Chesterfield Central Station.

The MS&L was not going to be content with just a line to Nottingham, since its chairman, Sir Edward Watkin, had conceived a much more ambitious objective. Also chairman of the Metropolitan and South Eastern companies, Watkin promoted a through line from Manchester and Sheffield to London and the Kent coast with a channel tunnel giving access to France and mainland Europe. To do so, the MS&L promoted its London Extension, opened in 1899, and transformed itself into the Great Central Railway at the same time.

Tibshelf Town Station, April 1950.

The London Extension rather confirmed the secondary status of Chesterfield in the Great Central's scheme, being off the main line on a loop and as such was closed in 1963 when all the local passenger services ceased; the through route closed to passengers from 3 September 1966. Watkin's channel tunnel was never built, the project waiting until the late twentieth century to be undertaken, by which time the Great Central line south of Sheffield had itself been closed and demolished.

Beighton – Langwith Junction

		Stations closed	Date
Passenger services withdrawn	10 September 1939	Upperthorpe & Killamarsh *	7 July 1930
Distance	12½ miles (Upperthorpe – Langwith Junction)	Spink Hill for Mount St Mary	10 September 1939
		Clowne South **	after April 1964
Company	Lancashire, Derbyshire & East Coast Railway (Great Central from 1907)	Creswell & Wellbeck ***	10 September 1939

* Named Killamarsh until 1 January 1907.
** Renamed as Clown & Barlborough on 10 September 1939; reverted to original name on 18 June 1961.
*** Named Cresswell until 1 September 1897.

Left: A Great Central 9Q class 4-6-0 locomotive, No. 37, at Cresswell & Wellbeck Station in late GC days.

The attractions of rail services into the northern reaches of the Derbyshire coalfield have been noted as the origin of a number of lines. An early railway connecting Eckington with the Chesterfield canal and the ironworks at Renishaw was followed in 1846 by the Sheffield & Lincolnshire Junction Railway, authorised in that year and opened in February 1849 between Sheffield and Beighton. This was followed after almost half a century by the line from Killamarsh to Clowne, opened in October 1898 by the Lancashire, Derbyshire & East Coast Railway, which connected with a line from Langwith Junction, near Shirebrook, opened in March of the previous year. Langwith became an important centre, connecting the Manchester, Sheffield & Lincolnshire to the LD&EC line from Chesterfield to Lincoln, the Midland line from Worksop to Mansfield and the Great Northern Leen Valley Extension line through Shirebrook South to Nottingham.

The LD&ECR ran through services between Sheffield and their own station in Mansfield, though in 1910 this amounted to only four return journeys on weekdays and a further two on Saturdays. Rationalisation in the Killamarsh area was prompted by the Great Depression in 1930 which saw the closure of Upperthorpe and Killamarsh station in that year, but it was the Second World War which saw off the remaining stations, which closed exactly a week after hostilities began. Unsurprisingly, goods traffic continued for several decades, finally ending in 1965, the route being largely duplicated by Midland lines.

Chesterfield – Lincoln

Passenger services withdrawn	3 December 1951	*Stations closed*	*Date*
Distance	37½ miles	Chesterfield Market Place *	3 December 1951
Company	Lancashire, Derbyshire &	Arkwright Town	3 December 1951
	East Coast Railway	Bolsover South **	3 December 1951
	(Great Central from 1907)	Scarcliffe	3 December 1951
		Shirebrook North ***	5 December 1964

* Named Chesterfield until 1 January 1907.
** Named Bolsover until 25 September 1950.
*** Named Langwith Junction until 2 June 1924.

Chesterfield Market Place Station, *c.*1906.

A flood at Bolsover Station, 27 July 1912. The locomotive on the coal train appears to be a Great Eastern 0-6-0.

The Lancashire, Derbyshire & East Coast Railway has already been described in the companion volume *Lincolnshire's Lost Railways*, which covered the eastern end of this ambitious project intending to connect Wigan with a new port to be built on the Lincolnshire coast near to Sutton-on-Sea. Chesterfield, which was in reality the western terminus of the 37½ miles actually built, was originally intended to be some way down the line from its point of origin in Lancashire. As it turned out, the association with Derbyshire was the only thing which gave the company's title any grounding in reality, the line to Lincoln being officially opened on 8 March 1897. The independent company was absorbed by the Great Central Railway in 1907 and they saw no need to extend it beyond Lincoln.

Coal from the South Yorkshire, Nottinghamshire and Derbyshire coalfields gave the line the bulk of its traffic, the passenger services being decidedly sparse, generally only four trains a day in each direction. These were cut back to Shirebrook North from Lincoln in 1951 and the entire line lost its passenger trains four years later. For many years after the bridges which carried the line into Chesterfield remained as local landmarks, though they were demolished in the 1980s. Some parts of the trackbed remain, though often these too have been obliterated.

A Class C 0-4-4T locomotive, No. 1150B, at Bolsover Station, 1919.

Right: Shirebrook North Station, 1965.

Pye Bridge – Mansfield *

Passenger services withdrawn	12 October 1964
Distance	9¼ miles
Company	Midland Railway

Stations closed	Date
Pinxton & Selston **	16 July 1947

* Closed stations on this line that were in Nottinghamshire were Kirkby-in-Ashfield East, Sutton Junction and Mansfield.
** Reopened as Pinxton North between 1 July 1950 and sometime after September 1961.

Though only a small town in the northern end of the Derbyshire coalfield, Pinxton attracted more than its fair share of railway promotions and schemes for routes, mostly never attempted. In 1832 the Midland Counties Railway had envisaged a main line from Pinxton to Leicester and Rugby, extending the existing tramroad from Mansfield. In the event the tramroad, opened in 1817 to connect with the Pinxton branch of the Cromford canal, was acquired by the Midland Railway – successor to the Midland Counties – and upgraded to a locomotive-worked line by an Act of 1847, the rebuilt line opening on 9 October 1849. Its coming allowed a great expansion of iron-making at Stanton, and also opened up the coalfield to the outside world. Coal and iron remained the staple traffics though there was a respectable passenger service, which eventually ceased in 1965. In 1972 a connection was laid to the former Leen Valley line of the Great Northern Railway at Kirkby-in-Ashfield to allow coal to be worked out from there.

Chesterfield – Staveley – Mansfield *

Passenger services withdrawn	28 July 1930
Distance	16 miles
Company	Midland Railway

Stations closed	Date
Whittington	4 February 1952
Barrow Hill **	5 July 1954
Staveley Town ***	5 August 1962
Bolsover ****	28 July 1930
Palterton & Sutton	28 July 1930
Glapwell	28 July 1930
Rowthorn & Hardwick	28 July 1930

* Closed stations on this line that were in Nottinghamshire were Pleasley and Mansfield Woodhouse.
** Opened as Staveley on 1 November 1888 to replace the first Staveley Station. Renamed Barrow Hill & Staveley Works on 1 February 1900; renamed Barrow Hill on 16 June 1951.
*** Originally Netherthorpe; became Netherthorpe for Staveley Town on 23 October 1893; renamed Staveley Town from 1 June 1900.
**** Reopened as Bolsover Castle on 28 July 1977 and closed again in 1981.

Situated five miles east of Chesterfield, Staveley developed in the early nineteenth century into one of the north Midlands' most significant centres of iron making. Early expansion had been helped by canals, but later the railways, principally the Manchester, Sheffield & Lincolnshire and the Midland, carried on the work and the town grew accordingly. As with other lines in the area, goods traffic (particularly coal) was far more important an incentive to railway building than passengers. The Midland's line from Chesterfield through Staveley and Pleasley to Mansfield was unusual in that much of it initially constructed as private industrial lines which the company then absorbed and upgraded, the final section between Bolsover and Pleasley opening to passengers on 1 September 1890.

The Midland's passenger timetable for 1922 showed seventeen trains each way between Chesterfield and Staveley, but only six from Staveley to Mansfield. In the event the passenger service to Bolsover lasted just a few months short of forty years, closing in 1930 at the height of the Great Depression, along with other lines in the vicinity. The section from Chesterfield to Staveley, which left the North Midland main line at Tapton Junction, soldiered on through the Second World War but nationalisation offered an opportunity to rationalise the passenger services to Staveley by closing the Midland route in 1962 in favour of the Great Central line. Sections of the route survived in mineral use into the 1970s.

Shireoaks – Mansfield *

Passenger services withdrawn	12 October 1964	*Stations closed*	*Date*
Distance	14 miles	Whitwell **	12 October 1964
Company	Midland Railway	Elmton and Cresswell **†	2 October 1964
		Langwith **	12 October 1964
		Shirebrook West **††	12 October 1964

* The closed station on this line that was in Nottinghamshire was Mansfield Woodhouse.
** reopened as part of the Robin Hood line.
† Named Cresswell until 10 April 1886.
†† Named Shirebrook until 18 June 1951.

Shirebrook West Station.

Mansfield, in Nottinghamshire, grew in importance during the nineteenth century, its prosperity secured by its place in the developing Midland coalfield. The Midland Railway began by connecting it both to Nottingham and to the Erewash Valley line, but in 1875 it ended the station's period as a terminus by constructing an extension northwards to the Manchester, Sheffield & Lincolnshire line between Lincoln and Sheffield, which it joined at Shireoaks Junction, just west of Worksop.

Closure to passengers came in 1964, but after being a freight-only route for thirty years a significant part of this line has been given a new lease of life as a passenger carrier by becoming the northern section of the Robin Hood line, linking Nottingham, Mansfield and Worksop. The line was reopened in stages from the south, Mansfield being reached in 1995, Kirkby the following year and Worksop in 1998. Further notes on the Robin Hood line appear in the companion volume *Nottinghamshire's Lost Railways*, but suffice it to say here that this is one of the more positive stories of Derbyshire's railways – a 'lost' line rediscovered. The original Whitwell station building has also gained a new lease of life. After closure it was carefully dismantled and re-erected at Butterley on the Midland Railway Trust's line, the original station there having been demolished after closure.

Manchester – Sheffield via Woodhead *

Passenger services withdrawn	5 January 1970
Distance	41¼ miles
Company	Sheffield, Ashton & Manchester Railway

Stations closed	*Date*
Crowden	4 February 1957
Woodhead	27 July 1964

* The closed station on this line that was in Lancashire was Manchester London Road (now Piccadilly). Closed stations in Cheshire were Guide Bridge, Newton, Godley Junction, Mottram and Broadbottom, and Dinting. Those in Yorkshire were Dunford Bridge, Hazlehead Bridge, Penistone, Wortley, Deepcar, Oughty Bridge, Wadsley Bridge, Neepsend, and Sheffield Victoria.

Although the Midland had a dominant influence over Derbyshire's railways, the Manchester, Sheffield & Lincolnshire was also a significant presence in the county. The London Extension has already been mentioned, but the company's original main line, linking Manchester with Grimsby and Cleethorpes, cut through the northern edge of Derbyshire. The route across the Dark Peak was the main line of the Sheffield, Ashton & Manchester Railway, which opened on 22 December 1845 and included the tunnel at Woodhead, just over three miles long and originally for single track only. After a few years traffic had risen to the point where a second single tunnel was required to ease congestion, but the two Woodhead bores were notorious because of their length and restricted size, coming at the summit of hard climbs in both directions.

The combination of the bleak moorland around Woodhead and the continuous gradients from Manchester made the line both a headache for operators a fascination to enthusiasts. The Great Central originally considered electrifying the line in 1913, but the project was postponed by the First World War. The LNER eventually decided to undertake the project and to construct a new double-track tunnel at Woodhead, but though work began in the late 1930s it was stopped for the duration of the war in 1939 and it was left to British Railways to complete the works. Construction of the new Woodhead tunnel began in 1949 and the line was opened throughout on 3 June 1954 as Britain's first fully electrified main line. Power was supplied from overhead line equipment at 1,500 volts DC and a fleet of 58 Bo-Bo locomotives (class EM1) and seven Co-Co EM2 type machines were commissioned to operate it.

No sooner was the route electrified than traffic began to decline; so much so that the Beeching Report of 1963 recommended closure with the remaining Manchester – Sheffield services transferred to the former Midland Hope Valley line. Passenger services were eventually withdrawn from 5 January 1970, but the line carried on as a freight route until 18 July 1981. Much of the trackbed remains as a walking and cycle path, but the 1954 tunnel at Woodhead has been re-used as a route for high-voltage power cables – a sad end for a project greeted with such acclaim just over half a century ago.

New Mills – Hayfield

Passenger services withdrawn	5 January 1970	*Stations closed*	*Date*
Distance	3 miles	Birch Vale	5 January 1970
Company	Manchester, Sheffield & Lincolnshire Railway	Hayfield	5 January 1970

Hayfield Station, 7 June 1958.

The section on the Midland's Peak line elsewhere in this book noted how the company gained access to Manchester in defiance of the London & North Western by an alliance with the Manchester, Sheffield & Lincolnshire Railway. The actual connection was at New Mills, on a line built by the MS&LR to reach the mill town of Hayfield. The line had a chequered history. Originally planned in 1846 by the Sheffield, Ashton & Manchester Railway, construction was commenced in the same year by the Manchester, Sheffield & Lincolnshire, as successor to the SA&MR. However, 1847 was the year after the speculators' bubble of the 'Railway Mania' burst and work on the line was halted by lack of capital in 1848. Nothing more was done by 1851 and poor traffic prospects led to the lifting of the track already laid beyond Hyde. Work began again in 1856 when the MS&LR hoped to use the route to gain access to Buxton, but this too came to nothing and it was left to a local company, the Marple, New Mills & Hayfield Junction Railway, to complete the line as far as Hayfield. In fact the arrival of the Midland route from Buxton in 1865 predated the completion of the line, the section to Hayfield eventually opening on 1 March 1868, over twenty years after it had first been planned.

Hayfield, situated on the edge of the Peak District and close to Kinder Scout, was a popular disembarkation point for walkers, who swelled the regular weekday travellers to and from Manchester. Between 1903 and 1912 the line handled much of the construction traffic in connection with the Kinder reservoir, and a 1½-mile standard gauge line was constructed to Booth Bridge to carry the materials, which were then transferred to a 2' 9" gauge line up to the works themselves. When the reservoir works were completed the line returned to its previous traffic levels and eventually goods dwindled to the point where facilities were withdrawn in 1963. Passenger trains continued until 1970, after which the line was closed completely beyond New Mills.

Closed stations on lines still open to passenger services

Nottingham – Derby

Company	Midland Railway

Stations closed	*Date*
Trent	1 January 1968
Sawley *	1 December 1930
Draycott & Breaston **	14 February 1966
Borrowash ***	14 February 1966

* Named Breaston until 30 June 1840.
** Named Draycott until 7 August 1939.
*** Replaced first station on 1 May 1871. Named Borrowash for Ockbrook between 1 May 1898 and 1 April 1904.

Trent Station, August 1960.

Trent – Derby via Chellaston *

| Company | Midland Railway | * The closed station on this line that was in Leicestershire was Castle Donington & Shardlow. |

| *Stations closed* | *Date* |
| Weston-on-Trent | 22 September 1930 |

Derby – Sheffield

| Company | Midland Railway |

* Named Smithy Moor until 1841, then Stretton until 1 October 1872.
** Named Wingfield (Alfreton), and subsequently Wingfield for Alfreton, between 1 December 1848 and 1 May 1862.
*** Named Sheepbridge & Whittington Moor between 8 October 1897 and 16 June 1951.

Stations closed	*Date*
Derby Nottingham Road	6 March 1967
Stretton for Ashover *	11 September 1961
Wingfield **	2 January 1967
Clay Cross	2 January 1967
Sheepbridge ***	2 January 1967
Unstone	29 October 1951
Dronfield	2 January 1967

Wingfield Station.

Sheepbridge & Whittington Moor Station.

Trent – Clay Cross (the Erewash Valley line)

Company   Midland Railway

Stations closed	*Date*
Long Eaton *	2 January 1967
Stapleford & Sandiacre **	2 January 1967
Stanton Gate	2 January 1967
Trowell	2 January 1967
Ilkeston Junction ***	2 January 1967
Shipley Gate	27 August 1948
Codnor Park & Ironville ****	2 January 1967
Pye Bridge †	2 January 1967
Doe Hill	12 September 1960

* This was opened to replace the first station of that name (400 metres due south) in July 1863.

** Named Sandiacre & Stapleford until October 1884.

*** This replaced the first Ilkeston Junction (260 metres due north) on 2 May 1870; it was named Ilkeston between that date and 1 July 1879.

**** Named Codnor Park until 17 November 1898; closed between 1 December 1851 and 1 January 1852.

† Named Pye Bridge for Alfreton until 1 May 1862.

Long Eaton Station, 1967.

Shipley Gate Station, 1948.

Trent – Clay Cross (the Erewash Valley line)